# *Men Are So Easy*

How To Tame Men Until They Will Eat
Out of Your Hand
And not Bite

In 10 Easy Lessons

Michelle Riley

Published, printed and bound
by Mike Riley
Aboard the Ketch Beau Soleil somewhere on the Seven Seas


sailingbooks@rocketmail.com


ISBN  978-0-9895532-9-2

This book is dedicated to my wife, Karen, who tamed me and who edited this book.


No Men were Permanently Harmed in the Writing of this Book

# Table of Contents

Scrunch up over here on the couch with me. Don't mind the petticoats. If you are wearing them that is. I hope not! Let's share a few secrets, Okay? Secrets are fun, aren't they? Let's share a few secrets about men. The truth is girls; men are so easy it is silly. Think about all the tears we cry into our pillows, all over men. Silly! And dumb! We are in the driver's seat, girls. Not that men have the slightest idea.

If fact, ladies, we can tame men to obey our every command easily. You can learn in only ten lessons, ten easy lessons. Why, they are so easy, you will be mastering men by tomorrow! You will be the envy of all your girlfriends. They will come to you with all their men problems. They will seek your advice. Yours! You better start practicing your superior but understanding look right now!

All your problems will be solved! Hurray! Life will be such a joy! Finally you will be able take a full breath and let it out, completely. Tension will be gone, joy will fill your heart, life will be so good! All because of these ten fun lessons!

Anyway, girls, buy this book, curl up with your pillow and change your life! This is the first day of a new and satisfying and exciting life!

# INTRODUCTION

# Men are all about Sex

Oh, stop complaining!  Yes, sex is all men think about.
What else is new?  That is the way God made them.  It
isn't their fault.  That is like blaming the male Praying
Mantis for being so involved in his love making that the
lady Praying Mantis can snip his head off and eat it while
he keeps on pumping away.  It is just the way God made
that species.  And don't go blaming Her!  My goodness,
She only had 6 days to make the entire universe.  Give
Her a break!  So what if she had to cut a corner here and
there.  It was a tough job.  She made Adam first.  And,
yes, I agree.  She gave him way too much sex drive.  But
why did She allow him to play with his sexual equipment
all day long?  It is so gross!  Yes, I know, he didn't have
Eve at first.  How could he even know what his goodies
were made for?

The way those men are always touching it, scratching it,
dare I say fondling it?  I really think that they would
rather lose an arm than their penis.  There!  I said it!
There is nothing wrong with using the proper name for
things.  In Biology class I would have been marked wrong

if I didn't use the proper name for things. Ladies. Let's make a deal among ourselves. Let's call things by their proper names during the lessons in this book. It will make things go much faster.

Men love their penis and balls. I suppose I should have said testicles, but 'balls' is so much more fun isn't it?

Every morning when waking, the first thing men do is reach down and pull their balls out from between their legs. They do! Wake up early and watch your man! Maybe it is some weird form of yoga. Salute to the Sun for penises! (Penii?) What would they think if we spent half the day scratching ourselves down there? They would call us sluts or worse. Life is so unfair. But then we don't spend the whole day long thinking about sex. We have more important things to think about.

Someone has to keep body and soul together. Someone has to do all the chores that make life a pleasure. Men don't do chores, or if they do, they do them poorly. I guess if they think about sex all day long, we can't expect them to do a complicated thing like sweeping the floor and do it well. To say nothing about vacuuming! Maybe that is why the lady Praying Mantis eats her man towards the end of sex. He wasn't doing any of the chores and the house was a mess. She is only going to make love once in her life, so why keep a useless man around? Besides, imagine telling him to lift his legs while vacuuming. All eight of his legs. OK, six legs and two arms if you are making a list. Some readers are so picky and say so endlessly in letters they insist on sending to me!

So, what can we do about this, girls?  How can we get men to behave, to behave without constantly telling them what to do?  Without turning ourselves in to nags and evil witches?  There has to be a way.  Some women have perfectly behaving husbands, boyfriends and/or lovers.  Why can't we?  How can we turn our man's constant infatuation with sex into a tool to influence their behavior?

That is what this book is all about.  I know, in fact all women know, men can't be changed.  However, we can get them to act civilized for a few hours, days if we are lucky.  Don't become too proud of your first success, for just when you are ready with a few words of praise, there they are getting out of bed, scratching themselves down there and looking out of the window at the girl next door.  Men!  Can't live with them and the cops take a dim view of us ladies chopping their heads off and eating them.  Maybe insects have it right.

Never fear.  After reading this short book, after studying these lessons, you will be in the driver's seat.  You will be the top honcho.  (Honcho-ess?)

Are you ready for a few secrets?  Here is a spare pillow.  Curl up with me.  I made a cup of tea for you and it is still hot.  Have a sip and let's open the book.

## LESSON ONE

# Men like to look at Porn

It is really a mystery why men look at porn. We women certainly don't need to. And anyway, why do they want to see a photo or a video of some slut when they have a real live woman right here? It is a mystery.

I caught my man looking at photos he had downloaded from the internet. I asked him what exactly he liked about each one of them. Boy, did I ever get an education! He showed me a photo of an 18 something with messy tangled raven hair, wearing nothing but lipstick. He said, 'this girl reminds me of you after we do it.' Another just showed her back and derriere. 'This one has a back just like yours when we do it doggie style.' Each photo had something to do with me! Then came, 'This one has legs like you could have if you walked more.' Arg! I let him live but it was touch and go for a minute!

My first thought was to take photos of myself. If he wants to look at naked photos of girls who almost looked like me, why not the real thing? My second thought was to start collecting photos of men with a six pack of abs.

I could tell him that this is what you could look like if you started exercising more! But that wasn't a very positive reaction. I didn't want to lower myself to his level. The idea is not to get even, it is to win the game, or at least gain the upper hand. But how?

Well, I had to admit that I dressed well when I left the house to go shopping or to work. I didn't take as much care when it was time to get between the sheets. Those girls in the photos must have taken hours before a mirror before they let anyone with a camera get anywhere close to them. I guess I could make a little extra effort.

Maybe if I tried harder, he might also. Fact is, he often forgot to brush his teeth before bed. In the morning, sure, but who has time for fun and games in the morning? Maybe if I tried harder, he might also. He might even double shave before he goes down on me! The luxury!

I decided to start going to the gym. It was an eye opener! Those gym-ites were really in shape! If I could look that good, I would be so proud of myself. Gee, I would strut around the bedroom showing myself off! And I might even catch my honey downloading my photo from the mantel instead!

# LESSON TWO

## Men like it when you scream during Sex

There you are in bed, making love, thinking about what to have for dinner as he is pounding into you and getting all sweaty and dripping it all over you. I mean how gross! And afterwards it doesn't even occur to him to wipe his sweat off your face and body. And we are supposed to love this creature from the black lagoon? UGH!

He certainly seems to be enjoying himself up there. He is grunting and everything. Every now and then he peeks down at you as if to make sure you are getting excited. Well, you are enjoying yourself. You have pretty much decided that Joy really shouldn't have worn that red dress at the party last night. And that Dave had one drink, if not ten too many. That hunk from Maintenance was wearing that see through shirt. You give a little shudder of delight. Your lover feels the shudder and increases his efforts. Unless he comes soon you are going to need major surgery down there! You give a little scream of terror. Your vagina is going to be so sore! His grunting reaches new heights. You give another cry of dismay that he mistakes for passion and he climaxes. Finally. Thank the Blessed Virgin. She had the right idea, who needs some guy pounding into you nightly?

Why not have your child virginally?   As if that could happen.  It would take a miracle!

Anyway, guys get off on hearing you being passionate, even if you are faking it.  You can get a hot reputation by faking it.  Of course sometimes you don't have to fake it.  Sometimes he gets it just right.

If you are going to fake it, fake it to your advantage.  If he likes it when you scream in "passion" get something out of it when you do.  If he believes that he turns you on, beyond belief, he will love and want you even more.  Convince him that he is Don Juan reincarnated!  I know it doesn't make sense.  If he thinks he is a regular Don Juan, you would think he would be out there populating the world, wouldn't you?

You and I know he is just a regular Joe trying his best, which isn't all that good.  After you convince him of his Don Juan-hood, any other girl he might try is going to be a disappointment to him.  One would think he would believe something is wrong with him, wouldn't you?  Guys aren't like that.  They really aren't.  He will be convinced that something is wrong with the other girls and that you are the greatest lover in the world, the only one that truly appreciates his love making.

Want to keep your guy at home in bed with you?  Scream while making love.  He will stay with you forever!

# LESSON THREE

## Men like sex when they are Bored.

Be careful, ladies. Don't fall into this trap. This is one step away from divorce. Sex should be a wonderful time. To turn it into something to do because there is nothing good on TV is a shame. Boredom sex is just one step away from him partaking in Prostitution.

All men will want boredom sex eventually in a relationship. Don't give in. Insist that if he wants sex that bad, he should start with kissing. Then tell him to eat you out. This is a road block. If he is really bored, he won't want to do it. He will be interested in his pleasure, not yours. Tell him that if he eats you to orgasm, you will give him a ride he will never forget. If he still insists, do some 69 or something with him. Whatever you do, make sure you both are panting with passion before you start the final act. If you do a really good job, he will forget when his TV program is due to start. Even if it is the playoffs. Gasp! Success!

Sometimes, you will get bored with sex. It is true, especially if your guy is an uninspired lover. When you become bored, he will sense it and become even more bored with you. Soon the two of you will drift apart,

maybe never to reunite or to have your love reignite.
Now is the time to have a brief, very brief, affair. Make it with someone who turns you on, most often someone younger. Although it is true that an older lover can teach you a lot about yourself. Make sure it isn't someone who you could fall in love with and perhaps more important, make sure he doesn't fall in love with you. You want an affair, not a prolonged relationship. You will feel your body become rejuvenated with the myriad possibilities of sex. Return to your lover with all these adventures in paradise fresh in your mind. He will ask, "What has come over you?" Just respond with, "but honey, you turn me on so much. I love you so much. My body aches for you so much. Please don't tell me that I turn you off." You aren't cheating on him; you are saving his marriage. Don't ever speak a word about your affair. Ever. It will be our little secret. Forever. Not even on your death bed. It will just hurt his feelings.

Ask him what you can do that will turn him on. Because you ask, doesn't mean that you have to do it. You are just opening an avenue of communication. Communication is key in sexual/marital relationships. Without speaking to each other, without a dialogue, your love life will be a series of one night stands. Uck! If he insists on you performing his desire, tell him that you have to think about it. He will translate that as he has to upgrade his bribes, his offerings of chocolate, flowers, dinner and movies, maybe even jewelry. And what is so wrong with that?

## LESSON FOUR

## Men like to chase new Tail

If you ask your man he will deny it, but it is true.  All men like the idea of pursuing new women.  Some men make a fulltime profession of it.   Watch your man as the two of you walk down a busy street.  When a young pretty girl comes along the opposite way, watch your guy.  For heavens sake, don't let him see you watching him!  All women have the ability to see out of the corners of their eyes. Men can't.  At least not as well as women.  Use that ability.  Watch your guy.  His eyes will follow this fantasy creature.  He can't help himself.  He is hardwired into pursuing women.

Now, here comes a young couple in love walking down the street.  Watch him.  He ignores the same woman your honey just checked out.  Does this mean that your man is getting tired of you?  That he is looking for someone new?  No, he isn't tired of you.  But, men love the idea of someone new.  Most men wouldn't do anything given the possibility of being alone with the new girl, but they sure do a lot of looking!  It doesn't make us feel very good, that is for sure.  Looking at other women, makes a man feel that he is still free; that he isn't completely oath bound to another, to you.  Yes, he is happy to be married to you, but still, he yearns for the idea of being independent.  Admit it now; don't you sometimes want to be free to flirt with some great looking hunk?  All women do, don't feel bad.  We are hardwired too.  Eve never would have offered Adam a bite of her apple if she hadn't checked him out first.

So, if he likes someone new, give him a new someone.  Dress up, act up, all women are born actresses.  Be one.  One day be a tramp, another a shy virgin.  Stay in character until both of you fall asleep exhausted.  If he really likes one character, bring her back now and then for an encore.

This is easy to do.  Playing a part for your lover is why God invented St. Vincent de Paul thrift stores.  She wanted us to have a wide assortment of costumes for our private acting career!

While we are on the subject, kind of, reward your man when he does something good for you.  Whether it is cooking a great meal or taking you out for one.  Cleaning the whole house for you or giving you a wonderful massage.  It is easy to reward him.  He wants sex.  Often he wants different kinds of sex.  No, he is not a pervert.

He is a guy. He grew up reading Playboy and Hustler. He thinks women are sexual animals. If he only knew that sometimes sex is the last thing on our minds! If he does a really great thing for you, reward him with the best sex of his life. You can have an amazing orgasm if the two of you come together. (Check out "How to Turn Your 60+ Man into a Red Hot Lover" by Mike Riley. It is also for younger men and for curious women.)

Training a man is not all that different from training a puppy. Use a smile, a kind word, a gentle hand down his back, and of course, sex. He will do anything for sex! It is the ultimate ~~dog~~ male cookie!

When that couple in love walked down the street ignoring everyone else, it was because they both were having so much sex that their minds were saturated. They don't want or need outside input. Give your man so much sex when he is good that he will never even look at another woman! And he is going to want to be good! Sex is the way to train men. It works a lot better than nagging and yelling. And is loads more fun!

## LESSON FIVE

# Men are all about Violence

Men love sports and the more violent the sport, the more they love it. Not just the blood and guts of football, but the hitting, smashing and running of baseball and tennis. The controlled whack of the golf ball, the aggressive ballet of basketball. Men love violence. Nothing turns women off as much as boxing; nothing turns men on more. Is there a connection between violence and sex? Is there a relationship between violence and sex and the way men practice lovemaking?

Some men like rough sex. Hollywood would like us to think that many men like it. Not true. Almost all men put their women on pedestals and like them up there. But still they like violence. They like violence in bed too, if you are the violent one! Yes, men like it when you are rough with them! Men love rough sex when you use them like a thing; like a toy! Really!

The next time you make love, get on top of him and use his body to get yourself off. Don't worry about him. Use him like an object. If he isn't hard enough, lean down and bite his nipples. He will stiffen up immediately. If he tries to fondle your breasts or nipples, if he grabs your hips to guide you, hold his hands down by his head. Don't worry. He will love it. Men love rough sex when he is the roughee. He will think you are one hot woman!

If he ever tries to get rough with you, if he wants his turn at bat, God forbid, take a page from his rants. Look at him right in the eyes, let your voice get all steely, (practice in front of the mirror first!) and say, "You want violence? Strip off all you clothes, now!" "Let me see that monster between your legs!" (More on this later!) "Get on that bed and spread your legs." Men are much better than vibrators and they don't need batteries!

Give him a few experiences like this and he will be in bed with you instead of watching the play offs or downloading porn!

More in the next lesson.

# LESSON SIX

# Men like it when you use them to Orgasm

It doesn't say anywhere in those books that he is in charge during sex. It doesn't. I should know, I read them three times! At least! Sex is supposed to be a coming together of bodies for pleasure, togetherness, and joy. Men usually start the ball rolling and take charge. Why? It is easy for men to orgasm. It is much more difficult for women to do so. Women should be in control. They really should. In fact, men like it when we use their bodies to orgasm ourselves. Weird but true.

Next time you are in bed, push him down and get on top. He will try to move his hips. Tell him to stop moving. He is ruining your concentration. Move around until you find the sweet spot. Start slow. Warm yourself up. Towards the end, let yourself go. He can help then, if you want. Peek at his face. He is watching you with great interest. He is learning what turns you on. He is having a wonderful time. When he comes, it will be a thunderous one. He really got turned on by you using him.

Let him come to grips that sometimes it is better if you are in command; that he will get more pleasure in life if you are running things; he doesn't know it but girls are better navigators that men.  They are!  No matter how many times we are turned around, how long we are blind folded, us women always know where home is.  Where the children are.  Somehow we always know.  The truth is She made Adam first and after She got all the kinks worked out, She made Eve!

When he does acquiesce to your being in command, don't waste it by telling him what clothes to wear.  Use it for VIS.  Very Important Stuff.  Like what car to buy, which party to go to on New Years Eve, or what clothes you should wear!

Once he gets used to the idea that you like to use his body for sexual pleasure, he will want to know how else he can give you pleasure.  Well!  He will want to do the dishes with you if whip his cute little butt with your towel once every few minutes.  With guys it is easy.  Any kind of attention is good.  He will gladly do the vacuuming if he thinks he might get to vacuum you.  If he actually tries, vacuum something between his legs, that will cool him down!

Take command at least some of the time in bed.  Gently, sweetly, take command of some of the rest of your life.  If you spice it with sex, he will go along happily.  All that men think about is sex.  Use it to train your man.

# LESSON SEVEN

## Men think of their woman as a Possession

So, is that all we are to them, slaves? They come to our beds and take us as things, slaves, as possessions? Where do those damn men get these ideas from anyway? Bastards! What should I use, a sharp knife or pruning shears? He is going to be so sorry!

Wait. My man does love me. I know he does. He buys me flowers and candy. He takes me to movies and out to dinner. He doesn't treat me as a slave. He doesn't.

On the other hand, he does refer to me as his wife. The bastard! Am I his possession? Am I his to do with as he pleases? Double bastard.

But wait. I do refer to him as my husband. I say that all the time; even in public. Do I consider him to be my possession? How cool! He is mine to throw on his back whenever I want to use his body! Yes! He is mine! All mine!

On the other hand, that is what I was just accusing him of doing and being. No wonder marriages have so many fights. They are really confusing.

Maybe we belong to each other. We are each a slave and a master to each other. We each can use and enjoy the other in love and in romance. We belong to each other only because we love each other. How cool is that!

No, no, wait. Just yesterday I was ready to kill him. He is the most annoying man in existence. An easy death is too good for him. Crucifixion, now there is an idea. But at times he can be sweet. Maybe marriage is a love hate affair. Equal parts love and equal parts hate. Does that make sense?

I guess emotion of either kind is better than boredom. If there is a death to marriage it is boredom. What if he was my possession and I was too bored with him to even acknowledge his existence? If I just left him in the cupboard all alone? A marriage based on fighting is better that being bored with each other, yes?

No. Don't give up the ship. You can create a marriage, a relationship, an affair entirely composed with only love. Start in bed. Carry the love you create into all phases of your life. If you find yourself wanting to yell at him for not doing some chore, go over and kiss him and glide your hand over his package. Work together doing the chore. Better than doing it yourself, getting angrier every minute. Tell him that if he helps you out doing the chore, you are going to screw his brains out!

Now, after, isn't that much more fun than yelling and screaming at him?

# LESSON EIGHT

## Men really like to Win

Men are competitive, very. While us more advanced women prefer to be nurturing and supportive, men haven't changed as the world matured. They are much the same as when they lived in caves and spoke in grunts. In fact they often still speak in grunts, sometimes repeatedly.

Their competitiveness isn't a problem as long as they aren't competitive towards us women. Men like to see who the top dog is in their tribe, and if it isn't them personally, they like to cheer on their team to win. With men, winning is everything.

This is fine as long as they aren't competitive towards us women. When they are, they can make our lives hell on earth. Most of us learned when we were still girls that we should ask fathers and brothers to open little jars for us. And then to watch with bated breath while they struggle to open a jar we could have twisted off in seconds. And, of course, to be ready with ahs and thanks when they finally do manage somehow. Set up a challenge and let them win.

In sports, men seem to think it is their purpose in life to score higher than us women. Don't they realize that we have better balance, better coordination, and more intelligence than they?

But the worse of all, if we are working girls, is if we make more money than they do. That really bothers them. Extremely. I don't know why. They started out to find the best wife they could, the prettiest, the smartest, the hardest working; and now they are complaining that we are using those same talents to soar in the business world. What is a girl to do?

First thing to remember is he isn't doing this to you personally. He is acting as his forefathers have through millions of years of social programming. Either that or as Adam taught his sons to act. Remember Adam wasn't the best father. His eldest son killed his brother. Clearly an excess of competiveness.

Personally, I don't see why your husband is complaining. With two sizeable paychecks coming in, life is so much easier. But he is resentful. The key is remembering that it is your money. Yes, you're married, it is both of yours. You earned it; you have a lion's share in saying how it is spent. Personally I think you should earmark your funds for family vacations. Really great vacations! Wouldn't that be fun? How can he complain?

Let him win when it really doesn't matter. But when it does matter, lower the hammer, girls. The poor sucker won't know what hit him. The idea isn't to win the battles; the key is winning the war. Compete seriously only when it is time to put him in his place.

## LESSON NINE

# Men will do anything to get Laid

What is it with men and sex? I mean don't they have a life? Does their whole life revolve around beer, sports and sex and not in that order? Wait don't answer that!

I like sex as much as any other girl. It is true that on some days (or afternoons) I like sex extra, extra a lot. But I do have a life, a life that doesn't revolve around sex. What is so wrong with men?

The truth is men got ripped off. Us women received a full two X chromosomes. Men got one X and a little tiny weenie little Y chromosome. The Y hardly has enough information in it to develop a little worm between their legs. That is it. We should not resent men's infatuation with sex. It is all they are capable of. They are just an advancement of a male Praying Mantis. Poor little men! I bet they wish they could communicate as well as we can. All they can do is grunt. True, some of their grunts are more exciting than others. The study of the sexes is so fascinating!

The best thing a girl can do is rather than fight against sex, join in! No, I am not promoting intercourse. Flirting is such a fun game. And a stolen kiss under the moon is so romantic! Two can play the game of sex infatuation!

Normally we are so quiet when we are horny. We just sit there next to him wondering why he isn't paying attention. Doesn't he know he has a horny sexy girl next to him? Doesn't he? The sad truth of it is, he doesn't know. When God was handing out insightfulness, men were last in line. No, strike that. Men weren't even in line; they were out tossing a football around with the apostles.

Unless he is horny we aren't going to get any action. It is a good thing he is horny so often, then! But it always seems he is never ready when we are raring to do it. What is a girl to do?

Communication is the key to sex. Good thing we women are talented communicators, isn't it? However most of the time, when we get that stirring, we freeze. We sit there like statues wanting it so badly but afraid to say anything. Time to take a page from men. They are never shy about their desires. I'm not talking about pulling down his zipper and sticking your hand in there, a kiss is all you need.

When you are turned on, your breath is laden with hormones. His primitive brain can sense these hormones and decipher their message, and act on it. Before you know it, he will be ripping off your clothes. Yippee!

Who knew that all it took was a kiss?

# LESSON TEN

## Men really like Compliments

Men are really simple creatures. If you want them to do something for you, don't jump in the sack, unless you want to that is, just give them a compliment. They really get off on verbal praise.

Don't use words like Honey or Sweetie. Yes that is what we like to be called. Men are strange and unusual creatures. Use words like; Hunk, Stud, Devil in the Sack, God's gift to Woman. There is no way you can lay it on too thick. They will eat up every word of praise, plus having eaten it, they will be putty in your hands until the next game is on TV.

Say things like: "Hunk, rub my back please. I am in the mood but I need you to set me afire. You turn me on so much." Watch him respond. Alter that to: "Stud, will you mow the lawn. Just the sight of your sweaty back turns me on so much. You make me want to be screwed by you. Turn me on, Hunk. Mow the lawn and make me melt." Remember, language is Eve's gift. She talked Adam into eating the forbidden fruit.

You can talk your man into anything by using a nice compliment. You can get your man to eat out of your hand by only using your vocabulary! Women rule!

# AFTERWARD

## Men are easy to Control

Men are so easy to control; it is amazing we have so much trouble. Remember when we were in High School and we played our favorite game? Told all the boys, 'Come here,' then, 'Go away.' And the boys would obey us; desperate for a kind glance from us, or a kiss, or maybe getting to first base. Now that those boys are men, they are more used to our ways. But we can still control them if we just make the effort and know how.

They are easy to figure out. Every thought they have revolves around sex. Even sports are but a way to become a hero so they can score some more sack time with a beauty like you.

Men love to look at porn. No one knows why. It is just the way She made men. Be sure to sneak some photos of your nude self into his collection. Make sure you take them just after a diet and after applying some make up. You are competing with 19 year olds!

Be passionate. Claw his back during love making. Scream when you orgasm. He will love it. He will think you are Eve reincarnate. Use his body to turn yourself on.

Pretend he is a giant vibrator!  Use him like a thing!  He will love it; strange creature that he is.

Life can be boring, especially if he has a boring job.  Don't let him take it out on you.  Bored sex is at the best, well, boring.  Don't put up with it.

Men love to chase women, especially new to them women.  Use your skill as an actress to become a woman of mystery for him.  He will stay with you forever.

If men don't get any, they might become violent.  Don't put up with it.  You are also a violent creature.  The Israeli Army had to stop putting women in the front lines.  After killing an enemy, they would stop, pull out a knife and mutilate him.  Not all women, but enough to freak out the men on their side.  If the case demands it, let your violent side out.  You can scare the bejesus out of him if you want.  Weird animal that he is, it will turn him on!

Do you think you are a slave, bound to obey, sworn to spread you legs at the merest command?  Men think you are.  They believe that once they marry you, you become their possession.  Bastards!  Beat him at his own game.  If he married you, then you married him.  He is your possession to do with what you want!  Use him!  See if he likes it. (Chances are, he will.  He will think you are one hot lady!)

Gamesmanship is a part of life.  It is a game that men play as if to lose is to die.  Don't let him play this game with you.  Don't let him control if you work or not.

Remember, you married him. He is your possession. He is yours to do with what you want. Use your wiles to get your way. Don't let him even think of winning the war, he can win battles if he wants, winning the war is what counts.

Men will do almost anything to get laid. Tell him if he jumps off the garage roof, you will jump his bones. Watch him go! We are the smarter of the sexes. We should be in control. Actually we are in control; all we have to do is offer the right bait. It is ours to offer. Watch him jump!

Men will do anything for a kind word from you. Who would have thought? And so easy! If he is shouting at you, say, "Stud, you turn me on so when you aren't shouting. And when you rub my back, I get so hot for you." Is that sexist? If so, so what? It works.

Men can be controlled. Men can be turned into, if not the perfect husband, at least one that can be lived with. Men are easy. Easy to control, easy to live with, easy to love. All it takes is understanding that men are all about sex.

_/) _/) _/)

www.ingramcontent.com/pod-product-compliance
Lightning Source LLC
Chambersburg PA
CBHW060602030426
42337CB00019B/3586